WHY ARE CANADIAN SENIORS WORTH MORE DEAD THAN ALIVE?

LEONARD H. GOODMAN

www.hereliesyourmoney.com
E-mail: info@hereliesyourmoney.com

Goodman, Leonard H., author
Why Are Canadian Seniors Worth More Dead
Than Alive? / Leonard H. Goodman

ISBN-13: 9780993819605 (pbk.)

straightspeak
A division of Yaantm Inc.
Toronto, ON Canada
www.straightspeak.com

Dedicated to Canadian seniors

TESTIMONIALS

"The Canadian insurance industry is big and powerful, and justifiably respected. But it is also very set in its ways and extremely reluctant to provide a policyholder benefit that is fair, and right, and accepted in almost every other country in the world: life settlements. Every baby boomer in Canada who has a life insurance policy should read Leonard Goodman's book, and once you've read it, you may well be motivated to get behind Leonard's crusade to make life settlements a reality for Canadians across this country."

James Deeks
Producer and Co-Host
TORONTO BOOMERS on Rogers TV

"Life settlements can, and should, be a key part of everyone's financial planning and they offer both life insurance policyholders and investors an excellent way of dealing with this valuable asset. It works well in the US and Europe and Leonard Goodman raises the critical question: Why not in Canada? In this easy to read book, he sets out the essence of the problem in Canada – a problem that should not be a problem. He challenges anyone with a life insurance policy to advocate for change saying if governments, insurance companies and financial planners work together to rectify this egregious situation then millions of aging Canadians will benefit, significantly."

Ralph E. Lean, QC
Toronto, Ontario

"Canadians can benefit substantially from a secondary, life settlement market for a financial asset that they own – their life insurance policy. Leonard Goodman's book demonstrates why Canadian life insurance policies are being devalued under antiquated, non-free market regulation that prevent the resale of a life insurance policy by its original owner for fair market value. This book will start a much needed conversation."

Brian T. Casey, Esq.
Corporate and Regulatory Insurance Lawyer
Life Insurance Settlements Association,
Board of Directors Member (2002-2013)
Atlanta, Georgia

"Leonard Goodman has crafted an insightful, easy to read, easy to understand guide book for anyone interested in life settlements."

Francine Wolfe Schwartz, President Creative
Consumers Services, Fort Myers, Florida

Alan, a sixty-four year old male living in the United States had a $500,000 life policy and through a life settlement he received a cash payment of $367,500—that's 73% of the full value of the policy.

From Life Insurance Settlement Association,
Orlando, FL., United States

A sixty-six year old female had a policy valued at $532,000 and received a $255,000 life settlement (47%).

From Life Insurance Settlement Association,
Orlando, FL., United States

TABLE OF CONTENTS

Millions of Canadian seniors are unaware that their life insurance policy is an asset that could be worth significantly more to them now if they chose to cash it in. It is their asset and yet they cannot get fair market value for it in Canada.

We have learned a great deal from the history of life settlements – the good, the bad and the ugly – and yet in Canada the benefits are buried under bureaucracy and intransigence.

FOREWORD

In this succinct, easy-to-read book, Leonard Goodman clearly explains the need for legal and regulatory change in Canada concerning a valuable financial asset held by many Canadians, life insurance. The book demonstrates why life insurance policies owned by Canadians, are being devalued under an antiquated, non-free market regulatory scheme that prevents the resale of a life insurance policy by its original owner for its fair market value. It is an important and serious issue and Goodman's book will certainly start a most needed conversation.

Leonard Goodman, over his long-tenured career, is an experienced financial and trusted advisor to many Canadian clients and in the early 2000s he was a participant in the development of the secondary life insurance market in the United States, which is commonly known as the "life settlement" business. I had the pleasure of working with Leonard and providing counsel on life settlement legal and regulatory matters.

Canada and the United States and their citizens have much in common. We both like hockey, fine beer and spending time in Florida during the winter, and now this book promises to serve as a call to action, putting Canadian and U.S life insurance policyholders on equal footing. Canadians, like their U.S. counterparts, should be able to realize the true value of their unneeded or unwanted life insurance policies that have served them well but no longer are a necessary part of their financial and estate plan.

The U.S. life settlement business had a meteoric rise within its tiny place in the financial products industry starting from its nascent predecessor, the viatical settlement business during the late 1980s and through the 1990s (set out in Chapter 2). It grew rapidly between 2000 and 2007 and yet today only a small fraction of the in-force life insurance policies have been "settled," and only a small number of life insurance agents know about, and understand, the life settlement business. Life settlements are akin to a "disruptive technology" in the life insurance industry, which doesn't happen often in this mature industry.

The disruption occurred not just in the sense of a rapid spurt in growth but also because it was a "game-changer." It challenged the long-standing idea that an unwanted life insurance policy could only be lapsed for no value (after paying years of premiums) or be "surrendered" to the life insurance company, in most cases, for an amount less than the policy's market value. It also challenged the notion that life insurance could never become an unneeded financial asset or be too costly to maintain after its purchase. Or that it shouldn't be a financial asset, tradable like any other investment that a person might purchase. Even the word "surrender," a term commonly used in the life insurance industry, implies that the life insurance company is the only proper purchaser of a policy, which is what economists call a monopsony. It also undermined the insurers pricing assumptions that over eighty percent of policyholders would allow their policy to lapse or be surrendered. However, with the life settlement of a policy, it is unlikely to lapse or be surrendered because it becomes an asset of an investor and premiums will be paid until maturity. This turned lapsed-based pricing on its head, exposing insurers to an unexpected, under pricing dilemma.

In a positive way, life settlements also changed the game for owners of life insurance policies, allowing them to obtain a market value for a financial asset rather than reluctantly surrendering it to the insurance company for an artificial value. Significant change came when life settlements caught the eye of investors in "alternative assets" who were looking for higher investment yields that had a low correlation to interest rates and the debt and equity investment markets.

All this disruption created a "perfect storm" for the formation of the life settlement business in the U.S. It resulted in years of legislative and regulatory change designed to address consumer protection: state insurance regulation for policy holders who might sell their policies and securities regulation for investors who might invest in the purchase of a life insurance policies. Eventually, the Internal Revenue Service also weighed in on the taxation of the sale of a life insurance policy. By and large the life settlement business in the U.S. now works well.

Canada can learn from this history and this book makes the case for such change. I agree with Leonard Goodman that Canadians can benefit substantially from a secondary market for a financial asset like this and it can be a "win-win-win" for everyone:

- Consumers: by enhancing their ability to maximize the value of unneeded life insurance policies that are their asset.

- Life insurance companies: by enhancing the liquidity of their life insurance products, making them more appealing to consumers because of a better exit strategy should their product retention need change and more saleable by life insurance producers.

- Investors: by permitting investments in a longer duration asset backed by high credit life insurance companies that can offset market risk accompanying traditional investment assets, further enhancing the value of life insurance products.

So perhaps this book will be the Chinook that facilitates regulatory change for Canadian life insurance policyholders. I certainly hope so.

Brian T. Casey, Esq.
Corporate and Regulatory Insurance Lawyer
Life Insurance Settlements Association,
Board of Directors Member (2002-2013)
Atlanta, Georgia, May 2014

PROLOGUE

Intelligence is not always knowing the answer.
It is always asking the question.

Maya Angelou

For most of us, the good ol' school days hold a trove of great memories and a stack of books full of lessons learned. I still have some of my old textbooks. But for me, it was some of the lessons learned outside the books that stayed with me over the years, and one in particular became a life-long principle. I remember raising my hand in a high school class and asking the teacher, "Can I ask a question?" His response was quick. "Leonard, don't ask, just ask." As a young student, what that moment and that teacher did for me was take the fear out of asking questions and it allowed me to learn the power of the question. From that day forward, I developed the habit of never hesitating to ask questions. And as a father, I encouraged my children to become incessant questioners. Once, one of my sons said, "Dad, I have a question but it might be a little stupid." My response was, "No, it would be stupid not to ask the question." I have found that the "eurekas" in life, big and small, come from asking the questions.

There are some critical questions about the life insurance industry that need to be asked and answered.

This book raises questions about an industry that I have been a part of for more than half a century. It is an industry I know well and I believe there are some critical questions that need to be asked and answered. Most of us are familiar with life insurance and, in general, we know that if we purchase a policy we might become worth more dead than alive. Of course, that is a primary purpose of life insurance but what most of us do not know is that life insurance can also have the potential to be of significant benefit to us while we are alive.

I believe there is a great injustice in the Canadian life insurance industry that is detrimental to millions of seniors.

Many people do not realize that their life insurance policy—an asset owned by them—could be worth substantially more than they think, before they die. It can potentially be worth much more than the "surrender value" the life insurance company would pay and something less than the full death benefit. And if the money is needed now rather then after death, then policyholders need to understand what is called in the insurance industry, "life settlements." In this book I explain life settlements and talk about what I believe is a great injustice in the Canadian life insurance industry and detrimental to millions of seniors. In the Canadian life insurance industry, life settlements are taboo and any hope of making them accessible to policyholders is locked up in the basement of industry bureaucracy, never to be talked about. What's even more perplexing is the fact that life settlements are readily available in the United States and Europe where they are well-regulated and there is a fiduciary obligation to inform the public of this option. This is not the case in Canada and not to address this difference is egregious.

What's wrong? Millions of Canadians with life

insurance are missing out on an opportunity to receive significant cash value for their policies while they are alive—if they need it or choose to. Canadians, Americans and Europeans have billions of dollars locked up in their insurance policies that they are not accessing, either because they don't know they can or they are prevented from doing so by regulations. Neither reason is acceptable. In the US and Europe, the regulations have been changed, awareness levels are increasing and millions of dollars in life settlements are benefiting people everyday. But in many Canadian provinces ... nothing. It is my hope that this book will begin to create a broader awareness of both the problem and the opportunity and lend a voice that advocates changing the outdated regulations that blatantly ignore the public good while benefiting only the insurance industry. As I like to say, 'It's time to put the life back in life insurance.'

This situation is contrary to the long-term needs of our aging population and the antithesis of a free market system.

I didn't arrive at this point without spending many years, decades, experiencing firsthand, the absurdity of the situation. In this book I relate stories of how life settlements have changed people's lives for the better and I also tell some disappointing tales of people who were prevented, by law, from selling their life insurance asset for much needed cash. This irrational, illogical and harmful situation must change because it is contrary to the long-term needs of our aging population and the antithesis of a free market system. It does not have to be this way.

A confluence of events brought me to this juncture. First, I am somewhat retired (my wife Alma might disagree with that assessment), and even though I still have a consulting practice for those who request my services, I have had time to look in the rearview mirror and also reflect on the road ahead. Looking back, I see life settlements as unfinished business for me and looking ahead, I see a resolution to the Canadian life settlement problem in the top-ten of my bucket list. Another factor, from a career perspective, is that my interests in life settlements can no longer be threatened by the possibility that my firm might be held ransom by life insurance companies and their self-serving point of view. They no longer have leverage over me, as Manulife Financial once thought it did when I became involved in life settlements a number of years ago. Back then, my firm was subject to sanctions and from that point forward, I decided I would only participate in life settlements in the United States and Europe, where they are acknowledged as an important consumer benefit and permitted and encouraged by regulation. Even then, when my involvement became known, Manulife Financial terminated my contract with them, citing, "failing to comply with Manulife Financial internal code of conduct." Ironically, their code of conduct does not seem to apply to Manulife corporately as they have been sanctioned on a number of occasions in courts both in Canada and the United States. I talk more about this double standard in Chapter Two.

The other reason I deferred writing this book until now is the fact that until ten years ago the life settlement business was in its embryonic stage, after emerging from the viatical business (covered in Chapter Two), which I did not condone. But since then, life settlements have proven to be a sound, secondary market and a well regulated industry providing real value to millions of consumers. All of these factors converged in 2013 and because this story had not yet been told in its entirety, I decided it should be. For the millions of life insurance policyholders who have the right to know and should have the right to sell their valued asset in a free and open market. My goal is to get the issues and the facts on the table so readers can ask the right questions and make informed decisions.

It's time for some answers.

Leonard H. Goodman

CHAPTER ONE

*You may be worth more alive
than you think*

*In this world nothing can be said to be
certain, except death and taxes.*

Benjamin Franklin, in a letter
to Jean-Baptiste Leroy, 1789

Even Benjamin Franklin didn't have it quite right about death and taxes because in this world some people do not pay taxes. But death … well, as Christopher Hitchens, a cancer victim, poignantly observed in his book, *Mortality*, we are "shackled to our own corpse … [and at some point in time, we move] … from the country of the well across the stark frontier that marks off the land of malady." It is not a matter of if, it is a matter of when, and life insurance plays an important role in how we approach life and death.

I have been affiliated with the life insurance industry for over fifty years and I know about the land of malady and inevitability and that it is the reason we buy life insurance. I also know that it is the place where life insurance companies make much of their money. It is a land they know well and yet most people do not know much about it and do not like to talk about it. Most importantly, what we don't know is that there is a particular point in our life when we are worth much more to the life insurance company alive than dead. And that point arrives for 80% of us on the day we allow our insurance policy to lapse[1]. Or we collect the pittance of the policy's surrender value from the insurance company. That is the day they have been waiting for since they sold us the policy. It is the day they pay us a small sum or nothing rather than paying out the full, much larger death benefit when we die. It is their secret and it is particularly true in Canada. I consider it a debilitating malady that affects—and infects—the well being of millions of people.

A life settlement pertains to the sale of an unneeded, in-force life policy for an amount that is more than the policy's cash surrender value but less than its death benefit. This is a valuable option for seniors who, for a variety of reasons no longer want or need to continue paying for a policy because its intended use may now be unnecessary or irrelevant. The surrender values paid by insurance companies are such that a purchase, in most cases by a life settlement provider (firm), can offer significantly more than the cash surrender value offered by the insurance carrier.

For many there is a cost-benefit squeeze between managing current expenses while maintaining a degree of post-mortem, financial security for beneficiaries.

A few years ago, I had a Canadian client (we'll call

him Sid) ask me about a one million dollar life insurance policy that his company had purchased some thirty years earlier. It was a "term-to-one-hundred" policy and it had been set up as key man insurance. He said, "Len, I'm eighty now and I just don't need this policy any more. And I don't want to keep paying the $18,000 annual premium." He asked, "What can I do?"

Millions of seniors in Canada are unaware that they could have a better option.

I remember thinking that Sid was in the same position as countless Canadian policyholders, facing the stress of ongoing expenses or certain life-changes. For Sid, it made no sense to keep paying out $18,000 a year with after-tax money and yet, if he stopped, the policy would lapse and be worth nothing (as a term policy). At age eighty, he was caught in an all too common, cost-benefit squeeze, needing to manage current expenses while maintaining a degree of post-mortem financial security for his family. Here he was with a significant asset that his firm had invested in and he was facing the possibility of receiving absolutely no financial value and no return until he died. This not-so-good-position is a serious—I suggest absurd—situation in the Canadian life insurance industry. Millions of Canadian boomers are unaware that they could have a better option: the opportunity to sell their policy in the secondary market, which is called a life settlement. Even in the United States, where they can do it, millions are still unaware of this valuable option.

I pointed out the first option to Sid. "You can do what most people do and simply stop paying the premium and let the policy lapse." I added, "And the insurance company will be most grateful because sometime in the future you're going to die and they won't have to pay the million bucks." Sid didn't like that option, which was basically "DOA," despite the fact that more than 80% of policyholders unwittingly opt for it. We talked at length and I laid out an alternative approach for his consideration.

Fortunately, Sid lived in a province that allows life settlements so we structured an agreement whereby I arranged for him to sell his one million dollar policy to a buyer who gave him $200,000 in cash and allowed Sid to retain a $250,000 interest in the policy until his death. The buyer owned the policy and agreed to take over paying the premiums until Sid's death. When Sid dies the buyer will receive the million dollar benefit and pay Sid's wife $250,000, minus 25% of the premiums paid. Needless to say, Sid preferred that option. He had $200,000 in his pocket now, plus he still had $250,000 benefit for after-death contingencies and he reduced his annual expenses by $18,000. If Sid had gone to the insurance company, they would have said something to the effect of: You have two options. Either reduce your policy from a million to say, $250,000 and the premiums will drop to about $4,500 a year. Or simply stop paying the premiums. Both, of course, are very much to their benefit. Also, Sid would not have $200,000 in his pocket.

This story is one of millions, very few of which have the same beneficial outcome. The fact that millions of Canadians (and Americans) are unaware of the hidden value in their life insurance policies is in itself a shame, but the real tragedy in Canada is that nothing has been done about it. Why? Two words: legislation and lobbying—ignoring the first and too much of the second. I delve into both of these in later chapters.

Life insurance is an asset that you own, just like
you own your house, car, boat or lawnmower.

For most people, life insurance falls outside the financial category that Warren Buffett was referring to when he said, "I want to be able to explain my mistakes. This means I do only the things I completely understand." With life insurance in Canada, the vast majority of people do not understand that there are regulations that prevent them from doing what Sid did even though their policy is an asset that they own, just like they own a house, car, boat or lawnmower. They can sell these other assets in an open market to the highest bidder but not their life insurance policy. The problem stems from three fundamental facts:

1) The self-serving interests of life insurance companies in Canada
2) Archaic Canadian regulations
3) People's lack of awareness of the value hidden in their policy

So far as reasonable safety permits, it is desirable
to give to Life Insurance Policies the ordinary
characteristics of property. To deny the right to sell
except to persons having such an interest is to

> *diminish appreciably the value of the contract in*
> *the owners hands.*
>
> Justice Oliver Wendell Holmes,
> Supreme Court of the United States

Whose policy, money and life is it anyway?
Over a hundred years ago, in 1911, the United
States Supreme Court, in Grigsby v Russell 222[2],
stated that it was constitutional for individuals to
sell their life insurance policy. It found that a life
insurance policy was an asset, no different than real
estate or any other item, and the owner had the
right to deal with that asset (within the law) as he
or she deemed appropriate. It is your policy and
you should be able to trade or sell it as you decide.
I go into some of the history in Chapter Two,
but the obvious and burning question is: Why,
after a hundred years, have things not changed
in Canada even though they have in the United
States, England and many European countries?
In Canada, "The true North strong and free …,"
we are not free from draconian regulations and
an entrenched, self-serving industry that prevent
buyers and sellers from freely converting the value
in their insurance policies. These rules and an
intransigent life insurance industry are shackling
consumers to an asset that can only be surrendered

for cash to the insurer, who predetermined the price many years earlier. It's wrong! It's absurd! It needs to change!

Why doesn't our government help level the playing field for seniors?

If Canadian provincial and federal governments took more of an interest in the financial needs of an aging population and the life insurance industry changed to meet those needs, millions of people could benefit. It begs the question. Why doesn't our government help level the playing field for seniors? Either they are unaware of the problem and potential solution or they don't care. One thing is certain, it's not going to change unless someone decides to change it and that effort is not going to come from the government or the life insurance industry without public pressure. In the United States there has been a strong consumer lobbying effort, state by state, and the industry has responded. We need the same in Canada. I might point out an irony with several Canadian life insurance companies. For example, Manulife, who also operates in the United States, must conform to U.S. legislation and yet, in Canada there is no such legislation but there is a strong industry lobby. The Canadian Life and Health Insurance Association (CLHIA) is a national organization that supposedly represents the industry at large along with its sister organization, the Life Underwriter's Association of Canada (now known as ADVOCIS), of which I was president of the Toronto Chapter in 1978. The problem is that most of the board members of CLHIA are executives of life insurance companies and it is not a strong consumer advocacy group when it comes to the matter of life settlements. Suffice it to say that CLHIA does not lobby for legislative changes that would help policyholders obtain a life settlement.

The burden of this imbalance on taxes and government and on the private sector could be crushing.

The issue of financial security and stability in an aging population is a critical one in every country and most of us understand the looming problem of the "boom and bust" economics, in which a large segment of aging boomers will have to be supported by a smaller cohort of their children and grandchildren. The burden of this imbalance on taxes and government and on the private sector could be crushing. Obviously, we need to do everything possible to mitigate this economic reality if we are to protect the quality of life for both aging Canadians and those destined to support them in one way or another. Today, retiring Canadians are carrying more debt than in the past and ever-rising costs continue to add to their financial load. They need more liquidity. And yet, maximizing the value of one of their most important assets—life insurance—is being prohibited. It is hiding in plain sight. The value available in life insurance policies through life settlements could be of significant benefit to hundreds-of-thousands, perhaps millions of people, especially now, when they need the cash—before they die. To emphasize my point, and my frustration, I like to adapt slightly Bill Clinton's famous 1992 campaign proclamation, "It's the economy stupid" … I suggest, "It's the insurance industry, stupid." In the U.S., seniors are receiving more than $7 million a day from life settlements.[3] That is a significant economic stimulus, particularly at a time when it is much needed.

A number of years ago, I was involved in providing a $20 million key man life policy for two senior executives of an American company. This is an example of something that is applicable to many people. Three years later they sold the company and called me and said they no longer needed the insurance. In the course of our discussion, I pointed out that they had another option versus cancelling the coverage. I showed them how, in the next five to seven years, the policy could be worth $6-8 million, as a life settlement. For everyone, the fundamental principle is: the value of your life insurance increases as your life expectancy decreases. Because the closer you are to receiving the full, face amount (the death benefit) the more it is worth, while you're alive. Of course, it depends on having the opportunity to sell it on the open market.

After our discussion, these two men decided to keep their policy as an investment with a plan to sell it later. In the United States, people are getting three and four times as much value through life settlements as opposed to cashing in on surrender value. If it were a term policy the insured would not have any value from the insurance company but could in the life settlement secondary market. This is particularly important when they need financial help while they are alive. Of course, many do not need this option but for those who have increased retirement costs, unexpected medical costs or other unforeseen expenses, the value locked up in their insurance policy could be … well, a "life-saver."

Things could change if Canadians knew about the hidden value in their life insurance policies buried under government apathy, industry self-interest and consumer ignorance.

Only in Canada

Let's take a brief look at the context in which I believe Canadians need to consider what is stopping them from accessing this valued asset. There have been many studies by financial institutions and governments (and I assume insurance companies) that set out the financial state of affairs of our aging population so I simply touch on a couple here from a May, 2013 CARP (Canadian Association of Retired People) article. They cite several studies showing that the average mortgage debt for homeowners aged sixty-five and older jumped by 8.6 per cent in 2012 and that uptick is more than three times faster than Canada's average 2.5 per cent increase for mortgagees from across all age groups.[4] But most have more than mortgage debt. Almost one in four Canadians over fifty with assets of at least $100,000, retired with outstanding balances on their primary residence.[5] A survey by CARP, a non-profit organization advocating for aging Canadians, showed that four in ten CARP members owe on more than just mortgages and the source was most likely a personal line of credit.[6] Susan Eng, vice-president for advocacy at CARP, says, "Because people now live longer and healthier lives, Canadians are more optimistic about being able to pay back their debts as they grow older compared to previous generations." [7] That's an important point and I suggest that people could be even more optimistic and capable of handling debt if they knew about the hidden value in their life insurance policy. In fact, if they were able to sell their policy they might have no debt. It is buried treasure, buried under government apathy, industry self-interest and consumer ignorance.

80% of the people will never receive the death benefit from their life insurance policy.

No one wants to outlive their money

It is up to "we the people," particularly seniors and their supporters. In Canada, the advocacy group CARP states its mandate as: "... to promote and protect the interests, rights and quality of life for

Canadians as we age." Life settlements certainly go to the heart of protecting the interests, rights and quality of life for aging citizens. The heading above, "Nobody wants to outlive their money," comes from the CARP website, where they state four primary goals, which, I suggest, align well with the intent of this book:

1) Freedom from excessive tax burdens and restriction
2) Freedom from predatory financial practices and consumer fraud
3) Adequate guaranteed income support programs
4) Equitable access to pension and retirement savings vehicles

The life insurance industry is heavily weighted in favour of the insurance companies, who calculate their profits, in part, by projections based on one glaring fact: In Canada it is estimated that 80% of life insurance policies lapse and are never paid and Life Insurance Settlement Association (LISA) has stated in one of its brochures that it is estimated as high as "90% of all policies issued lapse before paying a claim."[8] It is called "lapse ratio pricing." It means that when insurers calculate the price of the policy, they take into account the assumption that 80% of the people will never receive the death benefit. You do the math. In any business, those are financial odds worth betting on. And that's what they do. They bet that the majority of people will stop paying premiums and allow their policy to lapse prior to death; thus, collecting little or no financial benefit. That's a business with casino-like odds and the house wins most of the time. If, by chance, you decide to stop paying premiums and sell the policy back to the insurance company, you will find that you receive only a small fraction of the face value or indeed of the fair market value. Here's why.

Let's say you bought a policy at age forty and are now seventy-five and obviously a lot closer to mortality. That means your policy is more valuable—closer to collecting its full value. And yet, the value you can get from the life insurer through surrendering the policy, does not, in any way, reflect the value that you could get on the open market. The problem with the "math"— for you—is that the life insurer predetermined how much they would pay you if you wanted to sell it back to them, no matter what your age. They set a price some thirty-five years earlier and although the value has increased over that period (as you get closer to death), the value they set has not changed. And you have paid 30-40 years of premiums so the surrender value hardly reflects what you have put in. In fact, it's been reduced by inflation. That greatly favours them. If you do sell it back to them, you are operating in a monopsony, which is a market that has only one buyer. It is like playing monopoly with just one other person, except you don't even get to roll the dice again. As someone once said, "It's like buying a car from Ford and years later when you want to sell, the only buyer is Ford." And they're buying the car at a price they predetermined years earlier. Fair? Hardly.

There is no open and competitive market in Canada in which policyholders can get fair value.

Let me be clear. In Canada, you can sell your policy to another individual (i.e., a parent to a child) but you cannot sell it to a business or professional group specializing in buying and investing in such assets. Therein lies the rub. There is no open and competitive market in which you can get fair value. Your children or another relative or individual can legally buy it, but if they are not able or willing to pay fair value, then you are unable to maximize the value of your asset. You are limited to the lesser of two evils: a) selling to an individual in a non-competitive marketplace, probably, receiving less then fair market value; or b) dealing with the insurance company whose only interest is having the premiums continue or paying a low surrender value, determined years ago. Or better still—for them—having the policy lapse. You're stuck. Stuck with a decision you made years ago based on your needs at the time but now facing different circumstances and yet not able to find a fair common sense solution. The problem in Canada is clear: neither insurers nor governments appear to be interested in providing a better option and their continued obduracy prevents you from dealing with this prized and valuable asset under the usual conditions of supply and demand in a free market system.

As it stands, under the Ontario Insurance Act a person or business group risks being charged with "trafficking in life insurance policies"[9] if they try to buy policies from individuals and give those sellers fair value for their asset—as I did for Sid (neither Sid nor I were in violation of any regulations because he was a resident of a province that allows it and the policy was purchased by an American firm).

As in Warren Buffet's principle that we need to "completely understand" something, I suggest that most people in Canada do not understand what they cannot do with their life insurance policy after purchasing it. And they can be sure the insurance industry is not likely to tell them about the hidden value in their policy. The absurdity is all too obvious. Let's say I offer someone, I'll call her Sarah, two options when she is buying a policy. Option one: Sarah, you can buy a half-million dollar insurance policy and if you still have it when you die the full amount will be paid to the designated beneficiary. However, if at any time you stop paying premiums, the policy will be terminated and you will receive nothing in return—perhaps a small surrender value. Or option two: You get a half-million dollars of insurance and when you die it is paid to the designated beneficiary. If at some time before you die, you decide you do not need the coverage you can receive a life settlement based on a calculation of the "value of your mortality." I don't think Sarah would hesitate; she'd pick option two— except she can't if she lives in Canada.

CHAPTER TWO

*History has been a slow
but good teacher*

*I am not a teacher, just a fellow
traveler who has gone this way before.*

George Bernard Shaw

Alan, a sixty-four year old male living in the United States had a $500,000 life policy and through a life settlement he received a cash payment of $367,500—that's 73% of the full value of the policy. There are many similar American stories. A sixty-six year old female had a policy valued at $532,000 and received a $255,000 life settlement (47%). And a fifty-four year old male received $190,000 on a $2 million policy. That is just 9.5%, but the cash in hand was much more important to him at the time versus the much larger after-death benefit.[10] Most people who take advantage of a life settlement are sixty-five or older and have a policy with a face amount of more than $100,000. In order to enact a life settlement, the policy's market value must be more than the cash surrender value and the value of a policy is determined based on three factors: i) the amount of the death benefit, ii) the cost of ongoing premiums, and iii) the calculated life expectancy of the insured. Generally speaking, the lower the premium and the shorter the life expectancy, the higher the market value of the policy.

Calculating the value of a life settlement can be complicated and it requires experienced professionals. It is a specific and precise calculation and should only be done by a life settlement underwriter and actuary; it cannot be done by financial advisors or insurance brokers. In the United States, financial advisors have a fiduciary responsibility to represent the client's best interests and usually they receive compensation for service in the form of fees or commissions. The key for any policyholder is to get the right help and ensure that those people are duly licensed and approved. Regulations do vary from country to country and state to state. Most settlements are conducted through a broker, who solicits competitive bids from life settlement providers. Once a life settlement firm has calculated the life expectancy and an actuary has calculated the value that can be paid, the broker can go to potential purchasers and obtain competitive offers. It is an open and competitive market. It is possible for an owner to engage with a life settlement firm directly but if the firm is the only bidder the insured may not get the most competitive bid.

Over the last four years more than $8 billion in additional funds have been provided to American seniors.

In the USA there is an advocacy and trade organization called the Life Insurance Settlement Association (LISA), which was formed in 1994 and is the oldest and largest advocacy organization in the life settlement market.[11] Its goal is to advance the highest standards of conduct for market participants and to promote education and awareness to consumers, investors and public officials. LISA represents more than 100 member firms including 2,500 professionals who are life settlement brokers, life settlement providers, institutional investors, investment banks, hedge funds, law firms and life settlement services. One of its main purposes is to advocate and promote a code of ethics within the life settlement industry.

LISA stated in 2013 that life settlements provide American seniors with more than $7 million a day in additional money and over the last four years more than $8 billion of additional funds have been provided to American seniors—despite the fact that millions of people are unaware of this lucrative option.[12] Life settlements have delivered 409%[13] more cash than the cash surrender value that people would have received from their insurance companies. LISA further states that if every consumer that settled a policy had opted for the surrender value instead of a life settlement, they would have each given up, on average, $304,000 of value per policy.[14] According to a report issued in July 2010 by the Government Accountability Office (GAO), life insurance policy owners received an average of seven times more in a life settlement than if they had surrendered their policies back to the insurance company.[15] This loss—this reality—is what millions of Americans and Canadians are unaware of. In Canada, it is more than unfortunate; it is egregious.

Conning Research & Consulting estimated the market in unwanted life insurance policies (available for life settlement) was valued at $16 billion in 2008. Further, the life settlements market was projected to grow to between $90 billion and $140 billion by 2016 from a baseline of $12 billion in 2007.[16] We do not have figures for Canada but if we apply the rule of thumb, ten percent formula, Canada might have an annual average face value of life settlement transactions of over $2 billion. Perhaps more, because the Canadian population is one of the most highly insured in the world. This secondary market for life insurance provides liquidity for a most important asset and it adds value to all life insurance for consumers. Needless to say, it offers a great opportunity for policyholders and great potential for investors—except in most Canadian provinces.

58% of people 60 and older say they're delaying retirement and 79% of those say it is because they can't afford to retire.[17]

A little history

Let me provide some context with a brief historical overview of the business of life settlements. In the early going it was a rocky road (like many new and innovative businesses in the financial sector), with operators from the distasteful side of the business employing less than honest practices and those from the investment side not completing accurate due diligence. Today in the US, England and Europe, governments and practitioners have put in place the necessary regulations that protect the public. But most of Canada remains on the sidelines with outdated regulations that prevent investors from participating and the regulations are not in the public's best interest rather they are in the life insurance companies' best interests.

A quick timeline:

- I mentioned earlier the U.S. case of Grigsby v. Russell (1911)[18] , in which Justice Holmes of the U.S. Supreme Court delivered the ruling on behalf of the majority of the Court that life insurance policies are an asset. Like all assets, policies are freely assignable for value.

- In the 1980's, the AIDS epidemic left many patients in need of money for treatment and the secondary market for life insurance, known as viatical settlement, helped thousands of patients by purchasing their life insurance policies and paying them much needed cash.

- In 1994 LISA was established to fulfill the need for industry regulation and professional standards and to promote the development, integrity and reputation of the industry.

- By the late 1990's, many American seniors became aware of the option in the secondary market to exit unneeded life insurance policies. People over the age of sixty-five were able to sell their life insurance policy and benefit with a cash alternative to surrender value or a lapsed policy.

- In 2001 the purchase of life insurance policies became known as "life settlement." It was a $2 billion industry providing people with fair market value for their unwanted life insurance policies. Regulatory agencies were taking notice.

- By 2005 the life settlement option had grown to a $10 billion industry in the United States and was regulated in two-thirds of the states.

- By 2008 the industry had grown to $16 billion and involved sophisticated companies and institutional investors with regulated life settlements expanding across more and more states.

Despite the growth, the public remains relatively unaware of the opportunity to benefit from a life settlement option.

Now, let me fill in some detail.

We've come a long way baby

The slogan, "You've come along way baby dates back to a 1968 Virginia Slims cigarette advertising campaign and it is apropos of nothing other than the line applies to the life settlement business and how far it has come since the 1980s. For example, I have a client who turned seventy-seven last year, who, in 1992, purchased through my office a term-to-one hundred contract in the amount of $1,750,000, with a zero-surrender value. It had an annual cost of $20,800, fixed for life. If he was to keep it to age one hundred and was still alive, the insurance company would pay him the face amount. But that was twenty-three years in the future and his circumstances today had materially changed. He recently completed a divorce settlement, his children had grown up and were self-sufficient and he was retiring from active practice in 2014. He asked me, "What should I do with this policy?" We considered making his children beneficiaries but they didn't really need it, although everyone can use an extra $1M or so. But the reality was, as he said, "I need money more now because the divorce was expensive." So we arranged to put in his pocket $500,000 in cash by having the policy purchased by a third-party investor. And since the policy is the asset of the insured, he has the right to deal with it in any way he wants. After due diligence, we transferred policy ownership to the investor and the investor/owner paid the purchase price. The client was thrilled to pick up a cheque for half a million dollars. The alternatives would have been to keep the policy or walk away and get nothing. This story represents the healthy value of life settlements, recognizing the inherent benefits in peoples' policies while they are alive. A number of years ago, it prompted me to coin and trademark the phrase, We put "life back into life insurance."™

The principle was that if someone was dying and they had money in a life insurance policy, payable at death, why not allow for some of the asset value to be available while they were still alive.

As mentioned, the concept of life settlements and its precursor, viaticals, came out of the United States in the 1980s. The general definition of viatical is: A policy that is sold for less than its face value but more than an insurance company would provide the insured, and with the insured having a life expectancy of less than three years. The three-year timeframe has changed since then but the essential meaning has not. It began with good intentions. The idea was rooted in the principle that if someone was dying of AIDS or cancer and they had money in a life insurance policy (their asset), payable at death, why not allow for some of the asset value to be available now, before death. It was usually needed to pay for health care. At that time, a couple of major life insurance companies were sympathetic to the problem—in the United States, not Canada—so they agreed that if someone provided legitimate medical evidence of their condition, the insurer would be prepared to pay, in advance, a percentage of the owner's life policy in order to make life a little more comfortable—put the life back in life insurance. The balance would be payable upon death if the owner continued to pay the premiums. Ironically, the Canadian president of Prudential Life Insurance back then was instrumental in the early stages of developing a solution to this obvious need and yet, almost three decades later we have not evolved to where we should be in Canada.

Soon nefarious business people were seeking out sick and ill people and offering to buy their insurance policies at a discount.

As with many things, there are the Ponzi and Madoff schemers in the world and they looked at this situation and posited that if an individual can take his anticipated tax return to someplace and sell it for a discounted amount, why couldn't someone buy these life insurance policies at a discounted amount? That was the beginning of life settlements road to infamy and its good intentions were undermined by the fraudulent practices of a few bad apples and the poor business practices of a handful of investment people, particularly in south Florida. Soon, nefarious business people were seeking out sick and ill people and offering to buy their insurance policies at a discount. Some people in need of ready cash said okay and the buyers took advantage of them, sometimes almost stealing the policies by purchasing them at huge discounts. There were cases of half-million dollar policies where the owner had a terminal illness, with perhaps six to nine months to live. Buyers might pay as little as $150,000, receiving the full death benefit of $500,000 in less than a year. This attracted third party investors. For example, at that time I had a wealthy client who had been approached by a Florida insurance broker asking if he was interested in investing in life settlements. This was before financial institutions got involved so brokers were approaching individuals who had money. He called me for advice. I told him, "caveat emptor" because it was an unregulated industry. There were no rules against this practice in Florida and it was like the Wild, Wild West. He never invested. The insurance companies, rightly so, frowned on this practice but only from a moral perspective. From a business perspective, they looked the other way and this continued for four or five years.

The other side

Other business-oriented people saw the value of the concept in its more pure and moral form and from an investment perspective. There was a 100 percent guaranteed return—depending on who the insurance company was— and it was an attractive yield and non-correlated to the vagaries of the markets. These are important factors for any investor. If it was priced properly and enough policies were owned, it could be an attractive investment opportunity. But again, nefariousness raised its ugly head. Investors began to encounter less than ethical brokers. These brokers would offer $150,000 for a policy that they knew was worth much more based on statistical analysis. Also, in many cases, they avoided going to the open market to determine whether there was a competing bid that might increase the payout to the owner. This created a conflict of interest or conspiracy and it was only slightly different from the viatical-to-life-settlements. It took advantage of people who couldn't protect themselves. The calculations were based on unrealistic life expectancies and unreasonable high interest rate projections, which impacted dramatically the buying price. Realistically, based on today's economy, an acceptable yield should be 7-9 percent, which would pay significantly more to the insured; however, back then, most sellers probably decided that some money was better than nothing and sold.

This took place mainly between the mid-to-late 1980s and early 90s. I first became aware of it in the early 1990s and realized that if a life settlement investment was established with good business practices, it could be a sound business model benefiting all parties. I carried out considerable research and that is when I discovered and joined the Life Insurance Settlement Association (LISA) in the United States and a similar organization in Europe. They are advocates and press for regulations to ensure the industry is credible and ethical and over time they have been quite successful.

We determined that as a credible, well-operated business, we could serve a needed purpose and be financially successful.

Doing the right thing, right

Growing out of this history, I became interested in developing a business model that would consider a policy range from 4-12 years. I coined the term, "vanilla life settlements"—vanilla meaning pure, plain, straightforward—to reflect situations where individuals in reasonably good health and without a terminal diagnosis wanted to dispose of a policy and receive more than the insurance company would pay, but less than the full face amount. We went to some actuarial and underwriting organizations and did our due diligence, determining that as a credible, well-operated business, we could serve a valued and needed purpose and be financially successful. We established stringent parameters: We would not be interested in the viatical market; we would only look at AAA insurance companies; we would only consider situations where a life expectancy had been provided by an expert life expectancy organization and we would allow certain contingencies for a margin of safety. From this we could price at a reasonable rate based on market conditions. At that time, a reasonable return was 7-9 percent (compared to the 18-25 percent by the 'robber barons'). We had many brokers reject our offers because the "other guys" were offering a purchase price of say, $280,000 versus our $150,000. We simply said, if they want to price at a ridiculous number, "You go for it. And good luck with that."

Of course, that came back to haunt the investors. For example, some of the mutual funds in the United States bought tranches of these policies that, in our estimation, were mispriced. In 2009, I was invited to a meeting with a hedge fund in New York that had a portfolio of twenty-two life insurance policies with a face value of $150 million. The fund wanted to know if we were interested in buying the portfolio. We did our due diligence and told them that we estimated the portfolio value to be $25 million. Two years earlier they had paid $65 million. I told them they had overpaid. This was not uncommon. Other large sophisticated investment banks had made similar mistakes. They bought portfolios on the strength of very thin evidence, usually provided by a broker who had convinced them to make the purchase. Institutions were interested for "retail purposes," that is to offer their clients a new investment opportunity. Generally speaking, they would purchase a $150 million portfolio and anticipate a yield of say,

20% over seven years. Institutions would then turn that into a bond offering for retail customers to buy at a yield of perhaps 8% over seven years, planning to make 20% and pay out 8%. Customers liked it because the bonds were backed by the bank and the banks liked it because of the sizeable spread and the fact that the policies were backed by insurance companies. The problem arose later when many people outlived the inaccurate life expectancy projections and the return was much less than 20%. Of course, the bank still had to pay out the 8% and the premiums. Some banks defaulted, as with mortgage-backed securities (this was pre-mortgage-backed securities). It was a form of arbitrage that was simply too good to be true. One of the problems, in addition to a lack of due diligence, was that they didn't know what they were buying and the brokers were padding the numbers because it meant they could get more money for their client and higher fees for themselves.

There were millions of dollars of product and because there was little or no regulation the greed factor created overpriced and over estimated values. Two main factors led to these mistakes: 1) The life settlement companies were quoting unrealistic mortality; and 2) the actuaries were being asked by the brokers to calculate unrealistic interest rates. For example, our internal underwriters often came in with a life expectancy 10-20 per cent greater than the external life expectancy providers, which could mean a premium payment schedule, on average, about four years longer. This would turn a good investment upside down. For example, the combination of a life expectancy certificate for 7.2 years and an expected 30 per cent yield, wouldn't work if people were living longer. It bankrupted many portfolios and small investors. Conversely, we adhered to strict guidelines and principles. We had a life expectancy provider do an assessment for us on every file (hundreds across the United States) and we had our own in-house underwriting. We gave the same files to our underwriters and medical doctors, who were also in-house, and asked them to give us the numbers as if they worked for a life insurance company. And in every case, we were well above the life expectancy numbers of the third parties.

If you don't know what you're doing,
you shouldn't be doing it.

This was late 1990s, early 2000s, and in the face of such poor business practices and the lack of regulation, we simply decided to wait it out. We knew the other guys couldn't succeed based on the way they were operating. We held to the maxim: In life, timing is everything. And true to form, it all turned upside down. But we then faced the old maxim, "once bitten, twice shy," in that we had trouble convincing the pension funds or banks that life settlement was still a good investment and that we had the right model. They had lost millions of dollars sitting with portfolios replete with people who hadn't died yet. And there were lawsuits everywhere based on misrepresentation. So when we said we're a life settlement provider, it was tough getting a hearing. And when the economy started going sideways and 2008 hit, everything cratered. From derivative swaps to the Wall Street debacle, our model got painted with the same tainted brush and we were beating our heads against a wall trying to do this on a global basis.

It can be a sound and valuable business.

At that time, the CEO of a large Canadian life insurance company directed me to a senior vice-president of John Hancock who, in turn, agreed that it could be a sound and valuable business. I told him that I could buy policies based on sound practices and build a portfolio that he could invest in. And it would also be a natural thing for his firm to buy back its own policies, thus, removing the contingent liability from their financial statements. He agreed a hundred percent but said they were sitting back because they thought the existing life settlement companies would self-destruct. I even suggested they do their own underwriting and assessment but they decided to wait it out.

In the early 2000s, nefariousness, disguised as entrepreneurship, came to play again, particularly in South Florida with its large, aging population. The Madoff-type operators decided that if they could find 75-year-plus people who could qualify for insurance, they might be able to convince them to buy a $10 million policy to which the broker would then pay premiums for the first two years. Two years is the standard incontestability provision of life policies. After that they would be free to resell the policy on a life settlement basis. So they tried it. They placed invitations in the newspapers for a free weekend cruise to the Bahamas for seniors in good health and over the age of seventy-five. The purpose of the trip was to find as many people as possible to qualify for "free life insurance."

All they had to do was lend them their body for two years as a means to a financial end, from which they would receive a significant benefit, at no cost. And they didn't have to die. What's not to like?

It went something like this. If I were the senior, they would approach me on the cruise ship. "Mr. Goodman, nice of you to join us. We're having a little get-together in the ballroom and would like you to attend. After a presentation that was probably similar to the timeshare pitches people get corralled into, the sales people would work one on one. "Mr. Goodman, you're in pretty good health so we want to make you a great offer at this stage of your life. If you will agree to submit an application for a $10 million life insurance policy, and you are approved, we will pay all the premiums for the first two years." And they added, "We will also name your estate as a beneficiary of 20 percent if you die in that period." At this point, it sounds like an offer I can't refuse. Then they deliver the kicker. "And after two years if you allow us to sell the policy to a third party, we will give you 20 per cent of the proceeds." I, of course, ask what they think the proceeds might be. They say, "Well, it depends, but it could be anywhere north of a couple of million dollars." By then I'm in and the rest of the chatter is just about the details. All I had to do was lend them my body for two years as a means to a financial end, from which I would receive a significant benefit, at no cost. And I didn't have to die. What's not to like?

The insurance companies were culpable, in part, because they never asked the right questions.

Then these entrepreneurs went to banks and leverage-financed the asset value by assigning the contract as collateral and borrowing to pay the premiums. Their rationale to the lender was simple: After two years we will sell the policy to a third party for at least 30 percent of its value (i.e., $3 million). From those proceeds we will pay the insured their 20 percent and pay off the loan. In the interim, you loan us two years of premium payments—like a line of credit—which could be as much as $500,000-$750,000 over the two years. Of course, the third parties who buy the policy are more than willing to pay 30 percent on a $10 million policy for a now 77-plus year-old person. The middlemen, the brokers, pushed this because they were making a lot of money with no risk for them. In addition, they would also make commissions on the sale of the policy that could equal 100 percent of the first year's premium.

The insurance companies were culpable, in part, because they didn't perform enough due diligence. When they got the application they might question why a seventy-seven year old was applying for $10 million in insurance but the brokers would give them a cursory explanation. Perhaps that it was an estate situation. But they never asked probing questions about the "estate" (as they do today), mainly because they were thrilled to be writing the business. The person was insurable and the premiums were healthy so they did the standard underwriting and if the person qualified they issued the policy. The fact that the person was insurable and had a normal life expectancy went against the grain of life settlements because the yield would be impacted. It didn't make good business sense but the brokers didn't care because they were not keeping the asset, that would become the third party purchaser's problem, which it did. This became known as stranger-owned life insurance (STOLI), in that they were buying or selling a policy on a stranger. After a while insurance companies started to look deeper into the process and began to ask the applicant if they had any intention of selling the policy to a third party within the next two or three years. This made it more difficult to submit an application without lying, which would be fraudulent. But that didn't stop everybody; the money was too big, the greed insatiable. It lasted for several years and a few of the Madoff-types went to jail. Also, with so many schemes, it didn't always work out the way it was supposed to because the marketplace was getting more sophisticated and policies couldn't be sold. They couldn't achieve the numbers they were predicting and the banks were often left holding the proverbial bag. These STOLI and "premium-financed" deals became quite litigious, especially in Florida.

Life settlements have had a rocky history but the outcome has been positive because it makes sense for everyone.

The rampant buying and selling activity was problematic from the get-go and compared to our model and the way it should be done, it was a disastrous business enterprise. In our model, as I said before, we were not interested in premium-financed and stranger-owned contracts. Out of a thousand submissions from brokers and after considerable due diligence, we might have qualified 15-20 per cent as being acceptable. We wanted a clean, pure "vanilla" portfolio. This is the only way to operate a viable life investment settlement business. In 2006, as Chairman and CEO of US based First Equity Benefits of America (FEBA), I wrote a letter to a LISA executive stating our position:

> *First let me be clear, FEBA has stringent parameters with respect to life policies that are acceptable for purchase. Our parameters exclude "stranger owned life insurance" (STOLI).*

> *We exclude them for a variety of reasons, most of which relate to commercial and business philosophy. Having so stated, we also exclude them because we are of the opinion that such policies, essentially purchased for re-sale into the secondary markets, fundamentally undermine the real value and purpose of life insurance and the value it brings to the economy and countless beneficiaries to whom the death proceeds are directed.*

> *Unlike the insurance industry at large, we do believe that an accurately structured life settlement can and*

does bring immense value, beyond that which the originating insurer is prepared to pay, should the insured person wish to terminate his/her policy during their lifetime. We all fully recognize the under valued, and in many cases nil value, an insurer is prepared to pay at surrender, even though the value of the policy has without doubt increased due to aging of the insured.

How can STOLIs be erased?

Very simply, the insurance applications should ask the question, "Do you intend to sell/assign this policy to a third party within the next "x" time period? If so, to whom? If the answer is unacceptable to the insurer, it may then decline to issue.

Life settlements have had a rocky history but the outcome has been positive because it makes sense for everyone and in the long-term fulfills an important need in the market. Today, life settlements are a solid growth business, except in Canada.

The 2008 debacle—timing is everything

We all know about the financial debacle and recession of 2008 and like many others, it impacted our business. By 2005, we had completed our research, spent $2 million on infrastructure and had about a thousand brokers, bankers and CPAs on our support team and we were set to launch our company, First Equity Benefits of America Inc. in the United States and Europe. In 2006, we had a great launch in New York and my friend, Tony La Russa, then Manager of the St. Louis Cardinals, was our featured speaker. I remember it well because Tony was fresh from having just won the World Series. Our operating principles dictated that we would only conduct business when it made good business sense. We asked brokers to bring us clients and told them that they would get a fair underwriting but we would not accept any questionable contracts. Some were not that happy because it would cut into their likelihood of doing much business but we had no intentions of being associated, in any way, with the wrong side of the business. We were off and running, until 2008 hit. Even deep pockets were being extra cautious so our funding dried up and although our model had proved sound, we put everything on hold. Since then, the industry in the United States has matured and it is well regulated and reasonable in its marketing, pricing and evaluation and for millions of people it has "put the life back in life insurance"—except in Canada.

CHAPTER THREE

O Canada… oh no!

Possession of and control
over what happens to your own body
is a fundamental right.

James Vlahos, New York Times,
August 10, 2012

In most of Canada, life settlements are viewed as illegal. As mentioned, in Ontario, under the Ontario Insurance Act, if someone were to buy one policy from another person it would be okay. That's one policy. But if they were to buy more than one policy they could be charged with trafficking in life insurance. That is the term used in the Ontario Insurance Act. In Canada, when you buy a life insurance policy you are basically limited to holding it until death do you part or "giving" it back to the insurance company for its nominal cash value (unless it is term) or letting it lapse. I suggest that the real "trafficking" is the unfair profiteering that the insurance companies are enjoying due to the silence on this issue.

The life insurance industry in Canada is benefiting by an estimated $1 million a day.

Based on the current growth and activity in the life settlement market in the United States, I estimate that the life insurance industry in Canada is profiting to the extent of $1 million a day from policy owners (i.e., applying a 10% rule—see below). This money currently goes to insurance companies' bottom line but should rightly be going to the policy owners. It is their asset, not the insurance companies'. Let me explain further. We can do a simple projection based on the United States numbers. Looking at the aged population in the United States and how much life insurance is owned (a matter of public record), we can use the general rule that Canada is approximately 10 percent of the US population and if the US is creating about $7 million a day in life settlements,[19] then in Canada, we're looking at $ 700,000 a day. Annually that's $250 million not being distributed to Canadian policy owners. And since Canadians are the most highly insured individuals in the world, it is probably more like a million dollars a day. I cannot state this as fact, but it is a logical extrapolation. Regardless of what the actual number is, there is a significant amount tied up in the intrinsic value of an asset owned by Canadians but controlled by, and falling to, insurance companies. This is primarily due to the fact that owners are unaware of the hidden value and the insurance companies are just fine with that.

I am not a Ralph Nader but I see the injustice.

There are several reasons. First, and generally speaking, Canadians are conservative, reticent, even apathetic toward the workings and machinations of big corporations and ineffective governments.

When they read about fiascos such as a billion dollars wasted by Ontario Hydro or an ill-conceived gun registry, they shrug and carry on about their business. They might say, "tsk tsk …" at the water cooler but they get on with life. So something like this insurance deception, which is under the radar, doesn't even get noticed; therefore, there is no pressure on the insurance companies or government to address the issue. Until there is wide public awareness, which in turn translates into advocacy and political will, nothing will change. I am not a Ralph Nader but I do see the injustice and my intent is to encourage advocates to pick up the baton and bring influence to bear on the appropriate authorities.

In the agent-broker business, all brokers have contracts with the life insurance firms they represent. In the old days brokers were locked in. Just like in baseball a player was contractually tied to his team and could not talk or deal with another team and had to go wherever they sent him. In 1969, Curt Flood challenged the 'reserve clause' in players' contracts, which ultimately led to what we now know as "free agency."[20] Flood was "black-balled" and never played again but it led to Andy Messersmith breaking the free agency barrier.

Similarly, in the 1960s life insurance industry, brokers could only quote their sponsoring company. So being the maverick that I am, I pioneered multiple-company representation as opposed to single-company representation. It was a fight—a big fight—but we prevailed as other brokers jumped on the bandwagon because they saw the merit in properly representing the needs of clients over the desires of the life insurance companies. Under the then requirements of the Ontario Department of Insurance, and other provinces, every broker had to have a license to conduct business with a singular sponsoring life insurance company. That changed so that brokers could license with as many companies as they wanted, which allowed them to present a wider range of products to consumers. But still, any life insurance company can terminate this license with or without cause. It happened to me.

On September 23, 2010, I received a letter that reflects the authoritarian and arrogated power that Canadian insurance companies hold. I received a letter from the regional compliance officer for Manulife Financial. It read, in part:

It has been determined that you are involved as a

senior officer of a life settlement company that promotes the sale of life settlements and viatical agreements. Life settlements or viatical agreements are financial vehicles involving the direct or indirect purchase of death benefits of life insurance policies of terminally ill persons, senior citizens or other persons with shortened life expectancies. [My note: That is incorrect]. *The settlement permits an investor or purchaser to be entitled to receive the death benefit when a life-insured person dies, by paying a discounted price for the policy while the insured is still alive. Manulife's business practice policies provide that under no circumstance are Manulife's advisors to engage in any activity that is in any way related to life settlements, regardless of registration or licensing. We encourage you to refer to Manulife's financial code of market conduct. Any recurrence of the conduct which is subject to this reprimand may result in contract termination.*

I was asked to acknowledge it, which I did, and that resulted in the termination of my contract after forty-eight years of association with Manulife. I said to them, in no uncertain terms, "take a hike." In principle, I believed they had no right to tell me, or any broker, what to do in a completely independent business. But that might not have been the case for a broker who was not as well established. That broker could have depended on such a contract. Consequently, he may have gone along and terminated his association with the life settlement services. And that wasn't all. They had the audacity to go even further. They claimed that they were no longer going to provide me any access to my clients' policy records. They took the position that these were their clients and that they would give the files to another broker who would contact the clients and say they were handling their file. I received another letter to that effect, which, in part, read:

> "... following the effective date of your contract termination, we will commence servicing those clients, holding Manulife's products, from our head office, and these clients will need to contact our head office for information. Please note that after the termination date of your contract, you will not have access to Manulife systems for client information."

I had served many thousands of clients, representing many hundreds of millions of dollars worth of insurance, and I had kept these clients current on all relevant issues for over 45 years. Now, suddenly I was told I couldn't respond to their questions.

Why? Because I had a business interest in the life settlement industry in the United States, which would provide these clients with an alternative exit plan, when and if the time came. Fortunately, I was able to work around this problem by having Manulife appoint my son Jamie, who was licensed by Manulife to act as advisor to my clients. So through Jamie I obtained the information I needed to continue to serve my clients. I don't think Manulife wanted to get in a fight because interfering with my right to conduct business would not likely have held up in court. I solved the need for access to client files but I didn't solve anything regarding the advancement of the cause of Canadian brokers if they wanted to effectively look after clients' needs in terms of life settlements. This is just one example of the unfair and undue power insurance companies have over the market.

Question: Why is it different for Manulife and its advisors in Canada?

In my discussions with Manulife, I posed a few probing questions. I reaffirmed that John Hancock is a subsidiary of Manulife and that Manulife has a significant presence in the United States, which means Manulife is subject to US regulations. I also established that in the United States, Manulife brokers, by legislation, have a fiduciary obligation to their clients to offer the life settlement option. So I asked the 'million dollar' question: Why is it different for Manulife and its advisors in Canada? They had no answer. Because they cannot answer it. Their lame attempt has been to say they are a different organization. They also said that their code of conduct was written before life settlements became acceptable in the US, about twenty years ago. My response was, "Maybe it's time you rewrote it." But so far nobody has bothered to look at it.

We can only light the fuse. It needs a strong consumer advocacy to make the changes.

Current state of affairs

In the insurance industry, the entrenched thinking and intransigence toward change is legendary—my stories are but a few—and any hope of initiating change will come only from consumer demand for change. As an individual broker, or representing many brokers, we can only light the fuse. It needs strong consumer advocacy. Here is another example of the industry's intractability. In response to an article in the Globe and Mail in which Manulife CEO and President Don Guloien stated the age-old cliché (I paraphrase), 'my door is always open,' I wrote two letters to Manulife in an attempt to address Manulife's attitude toward me and life settlements; one on May 26, 2012 to Ms. Gail Cook-Bennett, Chair of the Board and the other two days later, on May 28, 2012 to Don Guloien,

Letter to Don Guloien,

I take the liberty of communicating with you directly for perhaps three reasons. First, I read the recent Globe and Mail interview you gave, and I was reminded, among other observations, as to the level playing field we all share in this life, irrespective of station. That in part came through from some of your comments, where you said 'my door is always open' basically. Second, I was further reminded of the access to your office that was frequently provided to members of Manulife field advisors by your predecessors, Alf Seedhouse, George Holmes and Syd Jackson, to name but three (three presidents going back over the years), who I was privileged to know very well and spend much time with. Dominic (Manulife's immediate past CEO) is another good friend. Thus, after almost a 50-year career, I owe Manulife a great deal of thanks. To be sure, my success came as a result of my own efforts, but in those past years there was usually somebody on Bloor Street who stood ready to support, assist and maintain an open door, from the very bottom through middle management and senior management. I take the liberty of enclosing my recent letter to Gail Cook-Bennett, Chair of the Board. This letter reflects my dismay at the loss of those 'good old days'. Personnel come and go throughout the years; I am saddened about what appears to be such a dramatic change in philosophy within Manulife.

I provide these comments respectfully.

This letter was never answered nor was the letter to the Chair.

Canadians are not well served by the life insurance industry's head in the sand attitude.

Within the industry, Manulife has always considered itself a pioneer and leader in Canada and the world, and yet it seems determined to suppress life settlements, which, as has been shown in the United States and Europe, can be very beneficial for consumers. I believe Canadians are not being properly served by this head in the sand attitude of the life insurance industry.

They are caught between a rock and a hard place.

What they are not telling you

I explained earlier how insurance companies price products based on a lapse ratio of about 80 percent and that they anticipate four out of five policies will be terminated, cancelled or otherwise disappear before the person dies, thus, avoiding any payout at death. In keeping with this thinking, they are opposed to life settlements because they know if a life settlement is transacted that the policy, after being sold as an asset by the initial owner, will not be terminated because the new owner bought it as an investment and will hold onto it until the insured dies. With life settlements, it would become zero-lapse pricing so insurance companies would have to either adjust their pricing policy, which they say would mean increasing premiums, or not permit life settlements. Obviously, in Canada, they have decided on the latter.

They are caught between a rock and a hard place. To come clean would besmirch their corporate reputation because they would have to explain why they are charging more. This would expose the fact that the pricing, over decades, was based on an 80 percent chance they would never have to pay the full face value. And they don't want that kind of information out on the street. They are reluctant to adjust their pricing ratios to compensate for the life settlement markets even though it is better for the consumers and better for the industry in the longer-term. I believe they should focus on the long-term value for the consumer. If a broker properly explains that if the full coverage is not needed in 20, 30, 40 years (and the insured hasn't died), then they will have an option to get a reasonable percentage of their money back, simply by paying a little more premium per month. What's wrong with that? And who wouldn't consider and probably take such an option? All the life insurance companies have to do is accurately price the policy.

I have a client, call him Peter, who is now seventy years old. When he was forty-five, he purchased a million dollar policy of term insurance. But rather then being a pure term policy, we added a provision, which cost him a few more dollars a year. Either after the age of sixty-five or twenty years, he had an option. He could cash in the policy and get all his money back ($200,000). Or if he wanted to continue he could maintain $500,000 coverage for life with no premium. Or he could keep the million dollar coverage and pay only 50% of the premium. No medicals required. It was his choice. So even though he would be paying slightly higher premiums he didn't mind because of the options he had later in life. Peter didn't need a life settlement because we had built the option into his policy, which was a better situation than what Sid and other clients faced. While most insurance companies offer pricing suggesting a zero percent lapse ratio, they are in fact, fully aware of the statistics that four out of five policies placed will not be in force at a time of claim. Simply stated, pricing could be calculated for the public on a much more attractive basis than it is. That is a major concern. And yet, they have no trouble increasing premiums. In fact, over the past five years they've been doing just that because interest rates are low and they're not earning as much on investments. But what they are not telling you is that life expectancies have improved and even as they increase premiums they are not giving policyholders a break because policyholders, on average, are living longer. Insurance companies are so myopic about the bottom line that they are avoiding offering consumers an alternative, which I suggest would be better for them and everyone in the longer term. As Alan Buerger, CEO and co-founder of Coventry Life Settlement company, an influential person in the US secondary market for life insurance, said, "I think the carriers are very short sighted and too many of them manage by looking in the rearview mirror instead of looking forward."

People would be buying their life insurance on a more favourable basis if they understood their options.

In a 2009 New York Times interview with reporter Joe Treaster, I said the complaints by insurance companies that higher premiums were costing them a lot of business were fallacious. I posited two answers: One, they would probably get more business because people would be buying on a more favourable basis if they understood their options. Secondly, I said they were complaining because they don't like the $10 and $20 million deals that are being accepted by the competition so they suggest a simplistic answer: Don't issue policies on a STOLI basis. This means insurance companies expect buyers to give up their right to go to the secondary market at a later date.

The insurance companies don't want to face a competitive market in which if one firm refuses to issue such a policy another will. So much for Adam Smith's 'invisible hand' in the life insurance market. Earlier I proffered the hypothetical example of Sarah and it is worth repeating. Let's put two potential buyers in a room. I say to one: "You need to buy a million dollars of insurance and when you die, if you still have it, they'll pay it out. If you terminate it or let it lapse, they're not going to give you anything. Or very little." I then say to the other prospect: "You need to buy a million dollars of insurance. If you die, they'll pay the million dollars. And if at some future date you decide you don't need it, they'll value your mortality (life expectancy) and give you perhaps two or three hundred thousand dollars back." Which is the better deal?

There's no one with endurance like
a person who sells insurance.

Let's go a little further with this overview. Generally, people tend to resist buying life insurance. People do not like to talk about their own mortality and there is such resistance that less than five percent of the brokers are successful because they do not have the endurance required when they meet resistance. Someone once said that there's no one with endurance like a person who sells life insurance. It is not seen as a tangible purchase and is bought primarily because of our inner concern for loved ones. It is often said that life insurance is not purchased, it is sold and because it is not a popular purchase there are frequent terminations due to buyer's remorse after the sale. Actually, life insurance is tangible and if properly explained it can be seen as a real asset. In essence, the purchaser is losing the use of some money (premiums) to protect loved ones who get it back after death. In the case of life settlements, the purchaser is given an opportunity to get some of it back before death, if they so wish. Except you know where.

Quite simply, the life insurance companies' motivation is to keep their short-term bottom line intact, which I consider short sighted because that does not provide the best value for the customer. And, in the end, customer value dictates long-term success. Right now, the 80% lapse ratio is working for them and it is such a lucrative cash cow that there is no motivation to change. But it hasn't always worked. A number of years ago, a Canadian life insurance firm introduced a term to age one hundred product that was a pure, no cash value, bare bones policy. If the owner died before age one hundred (the maturity), the beneficiary received the face value. If the owner and insured did not die but lived to age one hundred then the owner received the full face value. The policy was established at, say age thirty and continued that way. It was based on mortality at that time and the company had priced it on an 80% lapsed ratio without realizing that most, if not all, of the people were going to retain the policies as much as an investment as life insurance because the price would never go up and the end result would be paid one way or the other to somebody. They saw it as a good investment. When the insurance company realized what had happened they quickly stopped selling any new product and the actuarial people responsible for its design were dismissed. Essentially, the policyholder could have had a million dollar policy at a cost of $2,500 a year for the rest of their life. Of course, such a policy makes for an ideal life settlement purchase if the owner needs cash today.

The only way to overcome the inertia is to get the consumer involved by going public and catalyzing an advocacy movement to offset the industry lobby.

So how do we get the Canadian life insurers to change? I think it would be useless to try and convince insurance executives to change because I've tried. The problem is the infrastructure. It is so bureaucratic and most of senior management are wedded to the old way of thinking. And even those who 'get it' and would like to see change, can't overcome, even at the most senior levels, the inertia. The only way is to get the consumer involved by going public and catalyzing an advocacy movement to offset the industry lobby. I remember thirty or more years ago, the federal government of the day decided in its wisdom that it was going to tax the proceeds of life insurance at death, which heretofore had never been considered as a taxable benefit. It never happened and the reason it didn't was because the life insurance industry spearheaded a lobby to abolish what was coined the "widows and orphans tax." The government backed off.

The need is tangible, growing and there is considerable value in the untapped asset of life insurance.

What about the government?

The real oversight is that no one is making an issue of this problem and yet, it affects millions of Canadians, many of whom are in need of some economic "relief." As stated earlier, there are many statistics that underline the urgent need for action on this issue. Equifax has reported that consumers age sixty-five and over are increasing their debt faster than any other age group, at a rate of 6.5%.[21] And a RBC poll indicates that 40% of Canadians over the age of 50 have some form of debt and 22% entered retirement with debt.[22] Also, many are deferring retirement. The need is tangible, growing and there is considerable value in the untapped asset of life insurance.

Unless somebody gives voice to those most affected, governments will continue to ignore the issue. If governments aren't pressed, nothing happens. And there is silence on the insurance side by brokers, financial planners and life insurance companies. The government is a group of a few hundred individuals elected by many people who could benefit from a change in the archaic regulations currently in place so if elected officials even sensed there was a movement afoot, they would listen. It requires broad consumer awareness and participation, particularly among seniors, which, in turn, can bring change to the regulations. And then the life insurance companies will have to act.

CHAPTER FOUR

*One good investment
deserves another*

*If calculus or algebra were required
to be a good investor, I'd have to go back
to delivering newspapers.*

Warren Buffett

Back in the 1980's the financial firm, E.F. Hutton ran an advertising campaign with the memorable line, "When E. F. Hutton talks … people listen." Today that same mantra fits Warren Buffett of Berkshire Hathaway. When he buys, people pay attention. Well, Buffett and other large investment firms invest hundreds of millions annually in the life settlement business in the United States,[23] which is testimony to the long-term value and stability of the secondary market for life insurance. It speaks to the veracity, potential and competitive nature of the market. Buffett has a private firm that buys life settlements and brokers bring business to it.[24] It is a good business.

I mentioned earlier that I had discussed the investment side of life settlements with the then CEO of Manulife and he agreed that it could be a sound investment for insurance companies. I had explained to him what I was doing and suggested we could collaborate because we had a good business model. As partners, my firm would purchase upwards of a thousand life insurance policies and they would be considered an investment portfolio and be rated in the bond market. They would likely garner, at a minimum, a AAA rating. We would ensure that all the required actuarial and medical research was done to establish an average life span of, let's say, 8.2 years. Not everybody will die in year one, and some will live beyond the 8.2 years. It's an average. Based on that and the value paid for the portfolio, let's say for example, we paid $20 million for it, every year we would fund the premiums to keep all the policies in force. Our actuarial and medical experts would have calculated that the portfolio should be fully liquidated in 8.2 years for the remaining face value, which in turn would result in a yield of, say, 9.2% per annum. The policies would be with AAA insurance companies and my firm would sell the portfolio to the insurance company for, say, a yield to be calculated at 7%. Then the insurance companies would hold them and earn an attractive yield and guaranteed income. Where the investing insurance company purchases a portfolio, which includes a block of its own life insurance policies, that firm is, in effect, removing from its books the contingent liability with respect to those policies. The CEO agreed that it would be a good investment for his firm but when he got back to me he said, "I can't do it here (Canada)." But he did tell me to contact a senior executive at John Hancock in Boston. As mentioned, I had the conversation but nothing materialized in Canada.

It wasn't about a good business decision it was about not rocking the bureaucratic boat.

Also at the time, I met with the deputy chairman of one of Canada's largest chartered banks who was so impressed that he said he'd willingly invest his own money into such an investment portfolio. But in big banks these deals aren't done on just one signature so it fell into the political and bureaucratic quagmire. The bank encountered resistance from the insurance industry and internal politics. Of course, it all made sense but no one was prepared to open the door to further consideration, despite the fact that it made good sense. It wasn't about a good business decision it was about not rocking the bureaucratic boat.

In many ways this investment is no different than that of a conventional bond maturing in ten years with an interest rate of 6 percent. In year one, any bondholder can decide that instead of waiting until maturity they will accept a lesser return and take cash now. The bondholder has the right to liquidate early and receive fair market value based on interest rates. Or it can be held to maturity. The same premise applies to life insurance settlement bonds, which can be liquidated at fair market value in the open market. Conversely, and unfairly, in most of Canada, they can only be liquidated singularly to the insurance company at a predetermined and unfair value. While this is not rocket science, it results in millions of seniors losing out on access to a valuable asset in the here and now versus in the hereafter.

It is a good deal

Throughout my career, I've always maintained that for a deal to be good, it has to be good for all parties. And for it to work for both sides, each needs to leave something on the table because if not, then someone is not satisfied. From an investment perspective, life settlements can be a good deal for all concerned. Investors have the ability to invest in a product guaranteed by the underwriting insurance company because at some point the policy will pay off and it is non-correlated to the vagaries of the markets. We don't know when, but we know it will (everyone dies). So with proper due diligence and a fair and equitable formula, a firm can arrive at a number that satisfies the owner and the purchaser—even the insurance company. For the investor, it provides a good return on investment (ROI) with little tax involved because the proceeds at death from life insurance are recognized as a "mortality gain" and we don't pay tax on mortality gain. If it is in a corporation or holding company, then that corporation can pay out a capital dividend distribution.

It doesn't fluctuate like the market;
it only goes up in value.

It is fairly straightforward. Once the owner of a policy decides to sell his policy, we begin the process of valuing it. First, we check the last few years of health. We don't need medical reports for the past ten or twenty years. Based on this report, we have experts determine life expectancy and when we have that number, say it's set at 7.4 years, we allow for an additional 10 percent, taking it up to 8-point-something. That's a margin of safety to mitigate life expectancy risk. Then we apply a fair rate of return, yield, (according to current market conditions), and have an actuary do the calculations. An investor is always looking for a better-than-market yield on comparable products and today the market yield on guaranteed certificates is one or two percent, whereas a life settlement yield is far better. It is a bond in that we are buying a major life insurance company policy that has a guaranteed payout. Unlike regular bonds, it doesn't fluctuate with the market; it only goes up in value because each year it gets closer to payment. It is an increasing-in-value bond, which is guaranteed to deliver its rate, after tax. That's a solid investment.

The seller knows and is clear on what is being sold and the purchaser knows exactly what they are buying.

The objective is to provide institutional investors with a portfolio of say, at least a hundred policies, preferably more, which requires a significant capital investment. In addition to a straight up investment, there are a couple of options. The policies can be packaged and sold to a pension or hedge fund or an insurance company. They can buy the portfolio to yield a guaranteed return over eight years. If the investor is an insurance company, it also has the ability of removing the contingent liability risk of policies from its financial statements, after provisions for contingent reserves. For the investors in the portfolio this is called "securitizing." It is similar to the practice of mortgage-backed securities. But there is a big difference. With recent mortgage-backed securities, investors had no disclosure as to where or what the underlying security was, in fact, the banks selling these securities did not, for the most part, understand what they were selling. With life insurance policies, the bundling and selling is similar but with one crucial difference, transparency. The buyer not only understands what he is buying but also knows who is guaranteeing the investment. Major insurance companies!

A life settlement portfolio can appeal to a pension fund that might have $150 billion in the market and wants some of that money in fixed assets. This is a great fixed, non-correlated asset. At the end of the projected 8.2 years there can be additional value. Some of the insured will have outlived their life expectancy so if the pension fund wishes to have the life expectancy seller purchase those remaining contracts back, it can; thus, mitigating the pension fund's exposure. For example, at the end of the eight years, let's say that out of the original one hundred contracts there are eighteen left and the original, average age was seventy-six years, which is now eighty-seven. The seller may purchase these contracts back at the end of the projected 8.2 years and retain them, knowing the insured(s) will die in the future. To apply the old cliché, it's a win-win-win: the pension fund, the investors, the insured.

It can start with a small percentage of the more than five million Canadian seniors demanding change.

How can something that makes such good sense, as admitted by senior insurance executives, not be done in Canada? The barrier is a combination of insurance industry intransigence and a lack of political will, which comes from a lack of public awareness and demand. This can change if even a small percentage of Canada's more than five million seniors demand it. Change starts with them.

Fair is fair, except in Canada.

Fair market value

Most people have heard the term fair market value and know that it is a fundamental principle in a free market society. When you sell your house you want to obtain fair market value. When you sell your cottage or boat, same thing. And so you should. With life insurance policies, it was established a long time ago in the US Supreme Court decision by Justice Oliver Wendell Holmes in Grigsby v Russell 222 that "to deny the right to sell except to a person having such an interest is to diminish appreciably the value of the contract in the owners hand."[25]

A life insurance policy is a valuable asset and the same doctrine should apply but it doesn't in most of Canada.

First, let us understand the generally accepted definition of fair market value within the context of the Income Tax Act–Canada (ITA):

The price a willing purchaser will buy from a willing seller in an unrestricted and open market, with neither party being under undue pressure.[26]

"Fair market value is the highest price expressed in terms of money or money's worth, obtainable in an open and unrestricted market between knowledgeable, informed and prudent parties acting at arm's length, neither party being under any compulsion to transact."[27]

Consider the following case history in Canada. A privately owned Canadian Controlled Private Corporation (CCPC) was winding up. The CCPC owned substantial life insurance, valued at a face value of $6 million on the lives of two executives. Together the policies had a cash value of $1 million. Two policies with equal cash value and equal death benefit.

At the time, the executives were in their early seventies, both retiring; thus, the reason for winding up of the CCPC.

The executives consulted with their tax, accounting and legal advisors. When it came to the life insurance policies owned by the CCPC, they were advised to cash them in for the approximate $1 million in cash. However, one executive decided to consult with an insurance and tax specialist. The first question the insurance specialist asked was, "Do either of you need the cash values at this time?" The answer in both cases was a categorical no. The insurance specialist went on to advise that the executives arrange to purchase the policies from the CCPC in an amount equal to the cash surrender value of his/ her own policy. He explained how each policy was a valuable asset that if not purchased would be terminated and the insurance company would be able to remove the $6 million contingent liability from its books.

This decision goes to the issue of fair market value. The accounting firm retained by the executives insisted that evaluations be performed on the policies by qualified actuaries, opining that they must be transferred at fair market value. The insurance specialist agreed that fair market value should be established but in Ontario there was no way of doing so because there is no "open and unrestricted market." In Ontario and other provinces, it is either the insurance companies' way or the highway. The insurance specialist prevailed over the accounting firm and each executive was able to obtain their own individual $3 million policy for personal estate purposes—a valuable asset indeed.

Conversely, if this situation had taken place in the United States and other parts of the world where life settlements are allowed these two executives could have investigated the secondary markets and found that the fair market value of their respective policies was, in fact, worth much more than the cash values. But in Canada the substantial underlying increase in value would have gone to the insurance company. Does that make sense? Is it fair? Or just? These are questions every policyholder needs to have answers to. Ask the questions!

Postscript

Following the completion of the aforementioned transaction, I, to satisfy myself, went to the US secondary market to see what the policyholders might have received as a cash value. Each would have realized at least $600,000 over and above the cash surrender value they would have received in Canada.

CHAPTER FIVE

David and Goliath

David shouldn't have won.
Or should he have?

Malcolm Gladwell, author,
David and Goliath

In Malcolm Gladwell's bestselling book, *David and Goliath*, Gladwell tells numerous stories of how, in many walks of life, the underdog became a winner against formidable giants and long odds. But, as he points out, despite the initial perception of overwhelming odds in favour of the big guys the odds actually favour the Davids. Because giants have chinks in their armour and cannot fully defend themselves. I see similarities in this Goliath-like problem in the life insurance industry. Canadian insurance companies are big and they do what they do because no one challenges them and they have done nothing to better serve their customers with life settlement options because they don't have to. Also, we know governments are like Goliath's army, marching to their own tune and not changing much unless forced to face the reality of a palpable voter uprising. Only when voters prepare for battle do they pay attention. Unfortunately, lobbyists incessantly spin their stories in government ears and the unorganized, public army of "little guys" (much larger in numbers but seldom coordinated) have difficulty getting their stories heard. If 'we the people' are to have any chance of defeating giant problems like this, we need advocacy groups to stand up like David and take on the giant—

in this case, a two-headed, industry-government monster. Not to stretch the metaphor too much, but my goal, my hope, is that this book will be one of the stones that arms David's slingshot and begins to mobilize the public.

The insurance industry is a behemoth and history has proven that it does not change much and currently there is no incentive to change these outdated rules. Change will only occur if the life insurance companies participate and they will only participate if the consumer leads the way.

Below is an excerpt from the Ontario Insurance Act. Read it and ask yourself: Why can't it be changed? It needs to be amended to allow for the proper and regulated "purchase of life insurance policies" under life settlement agreements, in order to provide a valid and beneficial option to over five million Canadian seniors and all future seniors. The answer for me is: There is no good reason.

Trafficking in life insurance policies prohibited

115. Any person, other than an insurer or its duly authorized agent, who advertises or holds himself, herself or itself out as a purchaser of life insurance policies or of benefits thereunder, or who trafficks or trades in life insurance policies for the purpose of procuring the sale, surrender, transfer, assignment, pledge or hypothecation thereof to himself, herself or itself or any other person, is guilty of an offence. R.S.O. 1990, c. I.8, s. 115.

Doesn't someone in the industry or government think it's time to change? Just because someone thought that "trafficking" in life insurance policies was a bad thing 20, 30 or 40 years ago, doesn't mean it has any legitimacy today. Of course, there's plenty of insurance company rationalization, lots of political lobbying, much government apathy and most important, a lack of public awareness about the untapped value buried under the status quo.

Ideas without action are just dreams

Let's look at what can be done because ideas without action are just dreams. There are numerous groups who should want to see changes in the regulations, from seniors and their families to corporate executives, life insurance brokers and politicians.

Awareness
First, we need broader awareness among those

most immediately affected, seniors. A change in the regulations could significantly affect the financial decisions of many aging seniors—tens of thousands, hundreds of thousands, perhaps millions—and they deserve to know that their life insurance asset and its inherent value could be available to them if they so wish. Until they are aware of the possibilities, they will not be fairly served by their life insurance company, their financial advisor, broker or the government.

Seniors and most boomers are participants in countless activities and there are many venues where they can be reached to learn about life settlements. Of course, there is CARP, the advocacy group for aging citizens, which has approximately sixty chapters and more than 300,000 members across Canada. This subject should be on CARP's agenda because it can spread the word among members and advocate to government. I will make myself available, when possible, if invited to speak to such organizations. Of course, there are other groups, some local, some national. Word of mouth, fueled by unlimited Internet connectivity, can start a nationwide conversation about life settlement and it is my hope that this book and our website (www.hereliesyourmoney.com) will do just that; be a catalyst for change.

It's good business

Before delving into specific actions, let me address the importance of life settlements in the business world. Earlier, in Chapter One, I told the story of the businessmen in the USA I advised concerning their key man insurance policies. After the sale of their company, instead of allowing the $20 million key man, term insurance to lapse, they held on to it and a few years later executed a life settlement and received proceeds of more than $7 million in exchange for a premium investment of under $1 million. Similar opportunities should and could be available to businesses and individuals here in Canada—if we change the regulations.

Action required: What can you do?

I assume, if you have arrived at this point in the book, that this inequity offends you, perhaps as much as it does me. That's good. Because nothing is going to happen if we don't take action and you are not likely to do that if you are not somewhat ticked-off. It won't take much and to make it easier, I have listed contact information in the appendices. I urge you to contact your local MP and MPP and ask: Why are you being prevented from accessing the fair market value in your duly earned asset? And contact your financial planner, broker and advocacy groups, they should be working on your behalf. Just get started—by phone, letter, email, in-person or all of the above.

Your broker

If you have life insurance, you have a broker who makes money from your policy so put your broker to work. Ask them what they know about life settlements. It is possible that they won't know much but it won't take long to find out. The Internet is chock-full of information. As mentioned, it is a booming business in the USA and Europe and your broker can contact the Life Insurance Settlement Association (LISA) in the USA by phone or go to their website. What's in it for the brokers? In the long run, it is a good business option that better serves their clients and can mean more business for them if they help get the regulations changed. Of course, the life insurance companies that they represent won't want to tell them much other than perhaps tell them not to get involved, or worse, threaten to cancel their contract. But they need to realize that when this does change everyone will benefit. It is in their clients' best interest. So contact your brokers and start the conversation.

Financial Advisors Association of Canada (Advocis)

Advocis, The Financial Advisors Association of Canada is the oldest and largest professional membership association of financial advisors and planners in Canada. They say they are, "The voice of Canada's financial advisors." Good. That means it is an ideal place to voice this injustice. If you have a financial planner or know one, contact them and ask if they can advocate for you through Advocis. The organization has over 11,000 members in forty chapters across Canada and they serve millions of Canadians. On their website, in their own words, they state they are "committed to putting their client interests first." By not having the ability to discuss, explain and contract life settlements when conducting financial planning for their clients, the financial planner is not, in fact, able to put "their client interests first." Advocis should want to eliminate this disadvantage and inconsistency. So contact your financial advisor and/or the nearest Advocis chapter (www.advocis.ca) and ask the obvious questions.

CARP: *Your Voice Is Our Voice –*
Our Voice is Your Voice
What a great advocacy statement. As a "voice,"
CARP certainly offers our aging population an
invitation to be heard. CARP is a national, non-
partisan, non-profit organization committed to
a '"New Vision of Aging for Canada." And they
have a very apt and principled statement:"No one
wants to outlive their money." That is an incisive
and compelling endorsement of the principle
inherent in life settlements.

CARP can be a strong advocate for investigating
why aging Canadians do not have access to this
valuable investment asset. Their website states:
"Our mandate is to promote and protect the
interests, rights and quality of life for Canadians
as we age." Need I say more? Advocating for a
full and thorough investigation of the current
regulations is an issue tailored to the goals of this
national association. CARP says in its mission
statement that it is "committed to enhancing the
quality of life for all Canadians as we age." Also, I
want to mention a couple of their objectives here:
i) advocating for social change that will bring
financial security, equitable and timely access to
health care and freedom from discrimination; ii)

ensuring that the marketplace serves the needs and expectations of our generation and providing value-added benefits, products and services to members. I cite here two of its 'financial security goals for ensuring financial security as people age,' are: "i) Freedom from excessive tax burdens and restrictions; and ii) Equitable access to pension and other retirement savings vehicles." The current circumstances surrounding the prevention of life settlements in Canada fit both these goals, specifically, "restrictions" and "access." Contact CARP today. The information is in the Appendix B

*There is a reason that the rules
haven't changed in decades.*

Government—it's personal

This is personal. It's your life, your asset, your money, so I suggest you make personal contact with your Member of Provincial Parliament (MPP/MLA) and your Member of the Federal Parliament (MP). You can be sure that this important issue, at least important to you, is not on their radar. There is a reason the rules haven't changed in decades. Elected representatives probably do not know much about this issue so the task is to make them aware. Then maybe they will act. I suggest starting with your MPP or MLA because insurance acts are provincially legislated.

It is no secret that what moves governments is votes and if they begin to realize that a significant portion of five million senior votes are ticked off, this will get their attention. And our voice will get a helluva lot louder if we include those fifty-five and up. Remember "Freedom Fifty-Five" from London Life? Well tell your elected representatives that you want some freedom from these punitive regulations.

A few facts

There is no need to do a lot of research before talking with your MPP, MP, financial advisor and broker. Simply raise the question about life settlements and let their staff do the research. You can send them a copy of this book and a link to our website **www.hereliesyourmoney.com.** Just get the ball rolling. Use the information in this book and some of the key facts and statements we have set out in Appendix A. It is all good content to start the conversation.

An important conversation for every family.

Talk about living

This is an important conversation for every family because it has implications for all generations. Discussions about life insurance should be part of financial planning and when anyone purchases a policy they own a valuable asset. In Canada, the value is diminished because the majority of provincial governments do not allow life settlements, thereby precluding families (and businesses) from realizing the full value of their life insurance policies before death. More and more parents are retiring without adequate financial support and often due to a lack of cash, the next generation has to pitch in and help. A life settlement can help relieve that burden and everyone owning life insurance should have an option to access their duly acquired asset.

The last word

We can have the last word and I hope that the words in this book are the beginning of increased awareness and action aimed at fostering a conversation that puts the life back in life insurance. Wherever there is an injustice, truth can prevail but the true story must be told over and over again until the guardians of the status quo change and do what is right. A self-serving life insurance industry and an uninvolved, lethargic government may appear to be a Goliath but when confronted with the power of the people—"the little guys"—they can be defeated. Because wrong is wrong and the odds can be surmounted if enough of us adopt the mantra of the memorable line from the 1976 movie, Network: "I'm mad as hell, and I'm not going to take this anymore!"

Never doubt that a small thoughtful group of people can change the world. Indeed, it is all that ever has.

Margaret Mead

Let's begin the conversation and ask the questions that will, indeed, change this egregious injustice and unlock the cash in your life insurance.

AFTERWORD

Goliath is a bully

A March, 9, 2011, Globe and Mail article titled, *Manulife unit battles U.S. life settlements' industry,* clearly illustrates the extent that life insurers are going to in the fight to prevent life settlements from benefiting policyholders. The article's reporting fully supports the case that the life insurance industry, and Manulife in particular, are working to sabotage the life settlement industry for self-serving purposes. And today, three years later, nothing much has changed, especially in Canada.

I quote from the Globe and Mail article:

> *"Now Manulife's U.S. subsidiary, John Hancock Mutual Life Insurance Co., is being sued in California district court for allegedly trying to stop customers from selling policies.*
>
> *The lawsuit launched by Coventry First LLC, a large life settlement firm that buys policies and often sells them to major institutional investors, alleges that 'life insurance companies, such as Hancock, are seeking to destroy the*

[life settlement industry] because they want to reap the profit from collecting premiums without having to pay death benefits.'

The suit accuses Hancock of using bullying tactics to retroactively terminate a policy that was sold. Manulife declined to comment on the allegations, which have not been proven."

Post-script: John Hancock lost the decision, was fined and criticized in the judge's decision.

Also in the article:

" ... a recent New York Court of Appeals ruling said it was legal for individuals to take out life insurance policies on themselves for no other purpose than to immediately sell them..."

The New York ruling is a negative for life insurers, 'since an increase in policies that are sold to investors in the secondary market will reduce insurers' profitability as the value in such policies is extracted and maximized by third-party investors,' Moody's said in a research note."

Another key point:

> *"Industry experts say it's extremely difficult to quantify the impact that the issue is having on insurers because of a lack of data.*
>
> *The companies would never tell us how much they make off of lapses."*

Of course, they will never disclose that information but what we do know is that 80% of the policies lapse without insurers paying out any death benefit. Anyone can do the math. The life insurance companies' "bullying tactics" reaffirm the magnitude of the threat that life settlements pose to their reaping of untold profits.

As I set out in Chapter Three, beginning in September 2010, Manulife employed similar tactics against me. And their arrogance and bullying are further exemplified by this excerpt from a letter sent to me by Lester Heldsinger, a Manulife Vice-President:

> *"Consequently you must no longer deal with any of the Company's clients in respect of the Company's products. In the circumstances you*

will not be offered a Servicing Contract. New representatives will be assigned to service your clients."

In the same letter:

"The Company's published business policies … prohibit the Company advisors from engaging in the described activities … regardless of licensing, registration or legislation."

The arrogance is palpable in the complete disregard for "licensing, registration or legislation." And the contradiction between referring to policy owners as "Company clients" and "your clients," in the same mouthful, is an indication of their contradictory logic and irrational position. They are hiding behind a faux argument about whose client it is when the real issue is about whose asset it is. And all the arrogance and bullying will not change that.

Now, in 2014, it is time for Canadian policyholders to take up the fight against the arrogance, bullying and egregious regulations that are costing millions of seniors tens-of-millions of dollars.

APPENDIX

Appendix A

A few talking points

What is a life settlement?

A life settlement is defined as: A financial transaction in which a policy owner possessing an unneeded or unwanted life insurance policy sells the policy to a third party for more than the cash surrender value offered by the life insurance company but less than the face value. The purchaser becomes the new owner and beneficiary of the policy at maturation and is responsible for all subsequent premium payments and collects the death benefit paid under the policy when the insured dies.

Why can't I get a life settlement in Canada?

I understand that in most parts of the world, including USA, if I wanted to cancel my life insurance policy, I could have my broker investigate options other than just giving it back to the insurance company I purchased it from and accepting whatever they have determined it is worth, which is usually far less than fair market value. I am told regulations force me to accept whatever the insurance company offers while I perhaps could receive much more in an open and unrestricted market.

Why do government regulations favour insurance companies?

I believe that the life insurance companies are being offered preferential treatment over me and other seniors. Due to current government regulations under the insurance act (s), I am forced to take whatever the insurance company offers even though the fair market value can be substantially greater. It is my asset so why am I not entitled to any increase in value through the years rather than that value accruing to the insurance company?

How can we change the regulations?

As my elected representative, I am asking you to raise this issue in the legislature and determine how we can change the unfair treatment that Canadian seniors face because of these archaic regulations that are completely in favour of the life insurance companies.

Why can I not access my asset value?

Life settlements provide people in the United States with a total of more than $7 million a day in much needed cash because they can access the value in their life insurance policy, their asset. What is the reason Canadian seniors cannot do the same?

Why are there no Canadian advocacy groups fighting for this injustice?

The Life Settlement Industry Association in the United States was formed twenty years ago (1994) and it has been instrumental in establishing life settlements in 42 states. Why aren't there similar groups advocating for seniors in Canada?

APPENDIX

Appendix B

Why Are Canadian Seniors Worth More Dead Than Alive?

www.hereliesyourmoney.com

CONTACT INFORMATION:
LISTINGS FOR YOUR GOVERNMENT
REPRESENTATIVES

Government of Canada

http://www.parl.gc.ca/Parliamentarians/
en/members

Ontario

http://www.ontla.on.ca/web/members/
member_addresses.do?locale=en

Quebec

http://www.assnat.qc.ca/en/deputes/index.
html#listeDeputes

Manitoba

http://www.gov.mb.ca/legislature/members/
alphabetical.html
Seniors and Aging Secretariat
http://www.gov.mb.ca/shas/index.html

Saskatchewan

http://www.legassembly.sk.ca/mlas/

Alberta
http://www.assembly.ab.ca/net/index.aspx?
p=mla_home

British Columbia
http://www.leg.bc.ca/mla/3-1-1.htm

Nova Scotia
http://nslegislature.ca/index.php/people/members/

New Brunswick
http://www1.gnb.ca/legis/bios1/index-e.asp

Prince Edward Island
http://assembly.pe.ca/index.
php3?number=1024555&lang=E

Newfoundland
http://www.assembly.nl.ca/members/cms/
membersalpha.htm

Northwest Territories
http://www.assembly.gov.nt.ca/meet-members

Yukon
http://www.legassembly.gov.yk.ca/seatingplan.html

ASSOCIATION AND ADVOCACY GROUPS:

CARP
http://www.carp.ca/

Advocis (The Financial Advisors Association of Canada)
http://www.advocis.ca/about/contact.html

Life Insurance Settlement Association (LISA) - USA
http://www.lisa.org/

ENDNOTES

[1] *Life Insurance Settlement Association,*
http://www.lisa.org/

[2] *grigsby v. russell 222 u.s. 149 http://scholar.google.ca/*
scholar_case?case=9405495298337520720&q=grigsby-
*+v.+russell+222+u.s.+149&hl=en&as_sdt=2006&as_*
vis=1

[3] *Life Insurance Settlement Association,*
http://www.lisa.org/

[4] *Retiring with debt, May 31, 2013.*
http://www.carp.ca/2013/05/31/retiring-with-debt/

[5] *Royal Bank Media Newsroom, April 26, 2010. Four-in-*
ten Canadians retiring with debt. http://www.rbc.com/
newsroom/2010/0426-debt.html

[6] *Retiring with debt, May 31, 2013.*
http://www.carp.ca/2013/05/31/retiring-with-debt/

[7] *Ibid*

[8] *A Life: Free Market + Innovation, Life Insurance Settle-*
ment Association brochure, 2013. http://www.lisa.org/

[9] *"Trafficking in life insurance policies prohibited."*
Insurance Act R.S.O. 1990, CHAPTER I.8, Section 115
https://www.e-laws.gov.on.ca/html/statutes/english/
elaws_statutes_90i08_e.htm

[10] *Real Satisfied Members, Case Studies.*
http://www.lisa.org/

[12] *http://www.lisa.org/*

[13] *Data Collection Report, 2006, Findings, p. 3*
*http://www.lisassociation.org/vlsaamembers/files/lisa_*
research_data_collection_report_2006.pdf

[14] *Ibid, Conclusion, p. 4*

[15] *A Road Map to Life Settlements, LISA. http://www.lisa.*
org/content/47/A-Roadmap-to-Life-Settlements.aspx

[16] *Sam Rosenfeld, Life Settlements: Signposts to a Princi-*
pal Asset Class,Wharton Financial Institutions Center.
http://fic.wharton.upenn.edu/fic/papers/09/0920.pdf

[17] *Many delay retiring, USA Today, Feb. 27, 2014, Nan-*
ci Hellmich. http://www.usatoday.com/story/money/
personalfinance/2014/02/27/delay-retirement-mon-
ey/5785373/

[18] *grigsby v. russell 222 u.s. 149 http://scholar.google.ca/*
scholar_case?case=9405495298337520720&q=grigsby-
*+v.+russell+222+u.s.+149&hl=en&as_sdt=2006&as_*
vis=1

[19] *http://www.lisa.org/*

[20] *Curt Flood, http://en.wikipedia.org/wiki/Curt_Flood*

[21] *Debt by numbers, Barrie McKenna, The Globe and Mail, Aug. 28, 2013 http://www.theglobeandmail.com/report-on-business/economy/debt-by-numbers-troubling-trends-in-consumer-spending/article14017219/*

[22] *Four-in-ten Canadians retiring with debt, Royal Bank Media Newsroom, April 26, 2010. http://www.rbc.com/newsroom/2010/0426-debt.html*

[23] *Judi Snyder, Affluent, http://www.affluentmagazine.com/*
articles/article/200

[24] *Ibid*

[25] *grigsby v. russell 222 u.s. 149 http://scholar.google.ca/scholar_case? case=9405495298337520720&q=grigsb+v.+russell+222+u.s.+149&hl=en&as_sdt=2006&as_vis=1*

[26] *Revenue Canada Taxation, Information Circular 89-3*

[27] *Ibid*

ABOUT THE AUTHOR

Leonard H. Goodman is President and Founder of First Financial Group, which for almost fifty years has been providing a wide range of services for clients: wealth management, life insurance planning, tax planning, succession planning and management consulting.

He is also Chairman and Founder of First Equity Benefits of America Inc., a US-based life settlements company. Leonard is a member of the Governing Council at Sunnybrook Hospital, Toronto, a member of the Board of Governors of the Mount Sinai Hospital and served as a director of the Mount Sinai hospital Foundation. He is a honourary member of the Canadian Memorial Chiropractic College, served on its Board of Governors and chaired the committee responsible for building its new campus. He was president of the

Toronto Chapter of the Financial Advisors Association of Canada (ADVOCIS) and was appointed to an Ontario Government committee, under then Finance Minister Lawrence Grossman, that was responsible for introducing a code of conduct and ethics and mandatory liability insurance for licensed life insurance agents and brokers.

Leonard's passions are family – his wife Alma and their children and grandchildren – baseball, and a mint-condition, 1979 sports car that he has had since the day he bought it new.

THANK YOU

I wish to extend my sincere thanks to my long time friend and client David Hughes. It was David who suggested that I tell this story and then urged and pushed me until I did. Any value that might arise to our Canadian seniors should also be attributed to David. They will owe him a debt of gratitude. And to my wife and best friend Alma, who has encouraged me to persevere while using her academic prowess in reading the manuscript countless times and editing it and offering insight. Finally, a thank you to the life insurance industry. During the past 50-plus years I have seen first hand, how the end product has rescued families and businesses from potential disaster following the death of a business partner or loved one. Now it is time to take "the next step."